My Life of Change
Speaking the Creative Word
Seed Grow from Dark Place to Light

A Word
Speak It Plainly

Covell Johnson

Fulton Books, Inc.
Meadville, PA

Published by Fulton Books 2020

ISBN 978-1-64654-580-3 (paperback)
ISBN 978-1-64654-581-0 (digital)

Printed in the United States of America

This book is dedicated to God's Word,
changing my life.

Contents

Acknowledgments

This book is the sum total of who I am and how God's Word changed my life to His purpose. I am grateful for the inspiration and wisdom of God's Word, which helped me transform my life. To my brothers and sisters, I hope and pray that this book will help you see clearly how confession can heal your life.

Thanks to Jesus Christ, my Lord and Savior.

Preface

This book is about a fragment of my life and how God helped me through hard times. It is about the changes I went through, speaking the creative Word of God over my life. My life changed for the better because I learned a new way of thinking about life. God rules over all things, and I had to get to know my Father, who created me and all things for his pleasure. The Word of God gave me life, not death.

Life can be full of ups and downs. As you read this book of ideas and prayers centered around God's Word, I hope you will see how the spirit of God can inspire you to seek Him in all things in life and know that anything with God our Father is possible.

Writing this book was the hardest thing I have done. Writing about one's life was not easy. People think they know you, but they do not know what has happened in your life. I had to look to Jesus to help me understand what writing a book is all about.

Give Ear, O Lord

Jesus said if we asked anything in His name, He would do it for us, and He would pray to the Father, and He should give us what I ask according to His Word, even the Comforter that He may abide with us forever, even the Spirit of Truth whom the world cannot receive because the world does not see Him or know Him, but He would come and dwell with us and should be in us.

My Beginning

Growing up was not easy for me. I was the baby of the family. There were nine of us in the house, and Dad and Mom were both growing up together with us. I remember we all went to church as a family.

When good things happen for us, God remembers our faithfulness to Him. So now we are all grown-ups and have families of our own.

When you are a child at six years old, you do not know life is going to throw a curveball. I was hit by a car in front of my parents' house. I was under the car wheel, and they had to lift the front of the car off me to rescue me. Because of the impact of the speeding car when it hit me, I had two broken legs. My head was busted open, and my left ankle was crushed under the weight of the car. God saved me that day. If it was not for the grace and mercy of God, I would be dead today and in heaven with Him. I was in the hospital for eight months, recovering, and doctors said I would not walk again. That was a bad report, but God had other plans for my life, and that is good.

Today, God has made me whole. I am walking, and I played sports as I grew up. Yes, I am a walking miracle every day, and God's grace is on me every day of my life. I give God all the glory for what He has done in my life today.

I wonder how my life would have been if I had talked to God about the dreams and visions I saw as a child. Would there be fewer challenges in my life? The many different writers of the Bible wrote as the spirit of God gave them the inspired Word to write through them. Clearly, we look to God and His Word for answers in prayer and for healing in worship and praise to Him only. God wants the best for us in every area of our lives.

We can see the calling on Jesus's life in Luke 4:18–21 that says, "The Spirit of the Lord is upon me, because he hath anointed me to preach the gospel to the poor; he hath sent me to heal the broken-hearted, to preach deliverance in the captives and recovering of sight to the blind, to set at liberty them that are bruised. To preach the acceptable year of the Lord. And He closed the book and He gave it again to the minister and sat down. And the eyes of all them that were in the synagogue were fastened on Him. And He began to say unto them, this day is this scripture fulfilled in your ears." Jesus is anointed to do God's will. We have faith to believe and receive God's plan for our lives too.

Why does God inspire people of all backgrounds to write? Let's look at Isaiah 55. When we seek the Lord, we will find him and the answer we need in our lives. Let the wicked forsake his way. When we give up the wrong things that we do, God will help us fulfill His purpose. Our thoughts betray us, and God said to cast down all imaginations and every high thing that exalts itself against the knowledge of God. God's thoughts are always higher and clearer than our thoughts. In Genesis, chapter 1, God said, and what He spoke was what He spoke. God is God all by Himself.

Can you see clearly the vision God has given you to walk in life? Growing up was hard for me at times. In school, people told me that I was not going to make it, but God proved them wrong. I became a track-and-field star and went to college on a four-year scholarship and became an all-American for two years, but still, things were not clear for me. I came home early from college. It did not work for me. Who said life was fair?

Habakkuk 2:2–3 says, "And the Lord answered me, and said write the vision and make it plain upon tables he may run that readeth it. For the vision is yet for an appointed time but at the end it shall speak and not lie: though it tarry, wait for it; because it will surely come, it will not tarry." God has a time for all needs to be met. God does speak to us, but we are not listening to Him. We must stop and listen to His voice. Lord, help us to listen clearly to what you are saying to us today.

The lesson God is giving to us is clear. But where does the dark and shaded side come from'? The devil. We have to obey God in what He says in Malachi 4:8–12. I will not write all of it, but you need to read it all because it is God's will to bless his people. "Will man rob God?" Yes, all of us have at one time rob God in tithes and offerings, and God says that we will be cursed with a curse. "Bring all the tithes into the storehouse that there may be meat in mine house, and prove me now said Lord." God wants us to be blessed. "I will open the heaven and windows and pour you out a blessing in your life." Look at this. "I will rebuke the dourer for your sake," God asks us to prove Him wrong, and some do, and some don't prove Him. God wants to give us the best and full reward of life when we give love to Him—10 percent of what we make, and 90 percent go to us. That LS a good deal to me. I was not a cheerful giver at one time, but now I give and give all to God so I can stay blessed in the field and out of the field.

I said at the beginning of my book that I was not a great writer, but God could inspire you by the Holy Spirit to what is in your heart. I hope so far I help someone go in this life.

Note—I give all power and glory to God, our Father in heaven—nothing but the blood of Jesus.

The question is "Do we trust the Lord?"

When I was a child, I trusted my mother and father to feed me and clothe me. I had parents who gave us love and committed to our growth in life. But when we grow up to be adults, sometimes, we lose trust. Life will sometime have you think at times, *Do I really trust them?*

We must ask where did we lose that father and mother love. In Psalm 37:3, God tells us to trust in Him. Do we trust Him, and are we committed to His ways? I do not know when or where I stopped trusting in God, for He is the only one we can count on when times get hard for us. Our parents may not be there all the time for us, but God says when you commit your way to His way, nothing is impossible for you. Delight yourself in the Lord, and He shall give you the desires of your heart. Where did you lose your trust and commitment to Him? He wants you to come back to Him and see where you laid it down. Trust will always be a big part of our lives. I know when I delighted myself in the Lord, He met me at the point where I left Him. God's love is deeper than we could ever know. His heart is always with us even till the end of life in this world. When people, including family and friends, leave us, remember, God will never leave us alone, and His love never fails us.

All of us have at times in our lives do things we regret, but God looks at the heart of man. Challenges do come up, and it is how we answer the call of good and bad. When I was a child, I had dreams all the time when I was home asleep in my bed. People would be thinking I was dreaming my little head off. No, but at times, the dreams seemed good to have when I was sleep, and then things changed. How many people know when you grow up, your mind and images change year after year.

Let's look at Genesis 1:26–27. "God said, let us make man in our image... So God created man in His own image, in the image of God He created him; male and female He created them." God is God. All things, even images and thoughts and dreams and visions, are from God Almighty. I believe when God gives you a dream or vision, it will inspire you and give you a clear direction. God gives inspired dreams and visions, but the devil gives false messages and images to get us off the right pathway to a clear picture of God's plan for us.

Do people like to take instruction from other people? Let's look at Proverbs 9:9–10. I am not going to write all of it but parts of the verse. "Give instruction to wise man." God says that when we ask of him for wisdom, he will not cast you out, and you will be blessed when you take direction from him. That is so good to know that God wants me to ask Him. We, as Christians, can receive revelation from wisdom from God to help us in everyday life. That is good to know. It also says that we can teach a just man, and he will be yet wiser. In asking and seeking God for direction, we can have a good relationship with one another. I can remember hating to ask for directions. It seemed so hard to do. Why should I ask them anything? They don't know. But if you do not ask, how can you get instruction for life problems that come up? Now as I have grown up, life will make you ask questions on what to do to help you live. Instruction comes from God to help us learn about life, and when we do ask questions in our lives, it gets clearer and clearer.

Note—hear instruction and be wise and refuse it not.

How many people know what they are the sons of God? That is a good question to ask yourself today. Romans 8:14 says, "For as many as are led by the Spirit of God, they are the sons of God." Now that is good to know. I am the son of God, begotten of Jesus for what he did for the world. He gave his life on the cross, and through that, we are sons of God. And when Jesus has risen from the grave, we received the sonship of God. Read what else it says in the verse, for you have not received the spirit of bondage again to fear. Jesus paid the price for us. God gave His only begotten Son, that whosoever believes in Him should not perish but have everlasting life.

When we receive Jesus, the fear of bondage goes out the window, but we have received the spirit of adoption, whereby we cry, Abba Father. That is so good to know. God loves me and you regardless of what we have done because when we come and receive Jesus, all things are made new. The devil will try to get you to give up on God's plan for your life but do not do it. Fight the good fight of faith.

I received Jesus at age twelve, but coming into the fullness of God's plan for my life was not easy for me. We all gave good days and bad days. All I know when it turned for me, I knew when it happened. For in my spirit, I knew, and I acted on it (faith comes by hearing and sharing the Word of God). The spirit itself bears witness with our spirit that we are the children of God. That is so clear that I am a child of God, and that Jesus paid the price for all of us—then heirs of God and joint-heirs with Christ. Clearly, we are always in His will. Begotten of Jesus, all we have to do is receive His love that Jesus gave.

This part of my life is very hard to talk about, for it was a hard and lonely part of my life, not knowing that our body is the temple of God and that God dwells in our body. When I read those verses in Romans 12:1–3, I was blown away that God lives in me right now.

That was powerful. "I beseech you therefore, brethren." Look at what God is saying to us. By His mercies, that we are to present our bodies a living sacrifice, and here I was fornicating all over the place—out of control in every area of my life that did not look good. And I wanted to change. So I went to the Word to change my life around. For 1 Corinthians 7 says, "It is good for a man not to touch a woman to avoid fornication. Let every man have his own wife and every woman have her own husband." Yes! I read this many times but failed to see clearly what it meant to be as a believer.

Let me go deeper. I was dating and I mean not for marriage. One night, we were in bed together, and something came in and laid down between us. I knew something was wrong. I got up and looked and saw her face change in front of me. It was an unclean spirit that was in bed with us.

But clearly, God's Word says, "Flee fornication and know ye not that your body is the temple of God and not your own." So as I write this clear picture of what sin easily beset me, I am healed even now. I am going on to say, "Be not conformed to this world: but be ye transformed by the renewing of your mind."

Clearly, in this chapter, God is speaking. You must renew your mind in His Word. Overcome what is easily besetting your life from His life for you. It is a fight every day. But God told me if I would give it to Him in prayer and act upon His holy Word, He would help me and take that ungodly desire out of my mind and body.

Every day, my prayer is that the Word of God keeps my body and mind clean. Prayer does work, and the Word does work when we seek God and His redeeming power.

Note—transforming your mind is not easy. But when we act on the Word, God will fill us up with His presence and newness of life in Him. The Word is the seed of God.

Well, I have had an inspiring and challenging life, but God, who loves me, did not give up on me. We all need to thank Jesus, the Son of God, for intercession for us to Father God. I thank God for helping me to live and not die in my sins. Jesus was put on the cross and paid the price for all people of color. We are all made from dust of ground, but when the blood hits the ground, we all are made new in his image, the second Adam, Jesus Christ, our Lord.

Jesus is the newness of all men's lives. Christ Jesus fills our body and spirit with power and strength to overcome anything in life. I am saying that we are new creatures in God. The old things are passed away. Behold, all things are becoming new.

In 2 Corinthians 5:17–21 (I will not write all of it, but some of these verses help me so much to know that God made me new again in Jesus.) That is so good to know and so clear. The old life I lived is over, and the new one begins when we give our life to Jesus. Now that is a good exchange. Our past is over. The new one will strut. Why? Because Jesus paid the price for us, and God says, "If any man be in Christ Jesus, he is a new creature." That is so good to know.

So when people you know remember your past and do not know the end of it, you can say that Jesus paid the price for you and me. We have victory in Him. "What love God has for His people that through Jesus who hath reconciled us to himself and hath given to us the ministry of reconciliation to God our Father." We do not have a past but a new beginning in Jesus. I am so glad that Jesus made me new in Him and no one else. The newness of life Jesus gave us is one that I will never let go of. He loves me. That is so clear and so right. Thank you, Lord Jesus. It is clear that Jesus reconciled the world unto himself, not imputing our trespasses to us, but forgave the world and reconciled us back to God. Jesus paid the price for us.

Well, as I have said from the beginning of this book, I am not a good writer as many others before me, but God has many ways of getting people's attention to reach and write for Him. But hearing the voice of Jesus is not as difficult as we might think. God is clear when He speaks to us. We have to listen to what He is saying to us. He wants us to receive a clear vision from God to help lead us to the promise of God. The Lord has all kinds of ways to bless us to prosper. He says, "Bring all the tithes into my storehouse, and I will open up the windows of heaven and pour you out a blessing." We all like to hear that part, and we go nuts about it. Clearly, the Lord has already blessed us. Let's look at Psalm 1:3. I say again, we must wait on God's timing for us to prosper—like a tree planted by the river of water. When we go before Him, we mess up God's plan for us.

We have God's spirit in us. What we speak out of our mouths will happen like God Himself spoke it. But we all have to get to that point, our spirit man. Do we have the same creative ideas like God? Yes, we do. I believe we do have God's creative spirit in us to change lives and become more like him. God called us to be the praise of Him, and this is one thing we have to learn by faith. Well, we know Adam gave it up. He disobeyed God in the Garden of Eden when he ate the tree of knowledge of good and evil. Adam did speak like God. What Adam spoke and the animals that were the name it was called by Adam speaking it out his mouth. God gave him dominion over everything in the Garden of Eden. Adam gave it up in his disobedience to what God said to him.

When I was a child, I always had a creative mind, speaking things out of my mouth. But I did not know the power of my words that came out of my mouth. When God begins to speak the Word in him, things happen. So we have the same power of speaking also. God helps all believers understand the creative word that is deep down in us. If only Adam had obeyed God, we would have been speaking, saying words just like God our Father from the beginning. Now that is good to know.

Curveball

I never thought that when I got married, I was in for the fight of my life. It was hard, very hard at times for me as a young man taking on so many different life curveballs. One day, you're up. The next day, what happened? Marriage is a ministry up to God. "Whoso findeth a wife findeth a good thing, and obtaineth favour of the Lord." Sadly, mine ended because when two people are going in different directions in life, the enemy of this world will come in to still, kill, destroy, and that is what happened.

God's Word says that if we forgive one another, he will forgive us. But if we do not, then He will not forgive your trespasses. Forgiveness is the key to unlocking the blessing of God in your life. We, as God people, cannot hold aught against anyone. Was it hard at times? Yes. But God's Word must be obeyed.

I have to look at myself in the mirror and say, "I am a better person than this. God put in me His spirit, and I am not acting like it." So I go to the Word of God to seek answers to grow up. In 1 Corinthians 13, it says, "When I was a child, I spake a child, I understood as a child, I thought as a child: but when I became a man, I put away childish things." Two wrongs do not make it right to keep forgiveness in your heart. "Knowing this, that the trying of your faith worketh patience." we must have patience with each other to make it work in life or marriage. "If any lack wisdom, let him ask of God that giveth to all men liberally, and upbraideth not." God's wisdom is what we all need in times of making destiny decisions in our lives.

God says, "But without faith, it is impossible to please Me," and that is true. We all have to come to Father God in faith. Believing what He has spoken will come to pass when we believe in Him as Lord and Savior. I set out in my life now to hold fast to my confidence in God's Word every day because, in doing so, God rewarded you for seeking Him in the most difficult decisions in life. "But without faith it is impossible to please Him for He that cometh to God must believe that He is a rewarder of them that diligently seek Him."

My Change

An author wrote a book called *Understanding Your Potential*. If you do not have this, you are greatly missing out on life. That book helped to tum my lonely life around 100 percent. I tell men and women to invest in this man's book powerfully teaching of your God-given potential that is hidden deep down in every person that lives on the face of the earth. I knew I had something down in me. I took this man's book to help bring it out, and that is big for me. I see clear on life, and it looks good to me. "I can do all things through Christ which strengthen me," and God shall and will supply all my needs according to His riches and glory by Christ Jesus. This is why I wrote this book for my purpose and potential in me.

Thank you, Jesus, for not giving up on me. I will not die with my God-given potential inside of me, and you should not either. God the Father had given you secret wisdom that he placed in you before you were born—to understand a proverb, the interpretation, the words of wise, and their dark sayings. The fear of the Lord is the beginning of knowledge, but fools despise wisdom and instruction. God's plan for your life is priceless. We all need God's plan to move forward in making a change in our lives. It is said, "Hear you, children, the instruction of a Father."

To get wisdom, we need understanding also. I pray that we miss not the wisdom of God that is designed for our life from Father God. "My son, attends to my words; incline thine ear unto my sayings. Let them not depart from thine eyes; keep them in the midst of thine heart." God's Word helps release the change we need as we call on Him.

The Word of Faith

God makes me out of nothing into something—one idea from God who can call things from the invisible to the visible world can change your life. Everything I have existed came out of invisible to the visible realm. God calls those things as they are. He wants to give the blessing that is our in invisible to visible realm to us believers. My prayer is that all of us ask God to help us get the purpose and ideas out of us so he can use it to His glory and praise. God gives us all ideas to put into action. Something that is nothing becomes something. People's ideas are not them, and God, who creates everything, wants us to bring his ideas from invisible to the visible world around us—like businesses, investments, and many other ideas that have come out of invisible to the visible.

Remember, God has you in Him before He speaks you out of Him. We are in God's ideas before he makes all things from nothing into something. So God has many ideas in Himself. Remember, if you have an idea to do something, the idea comes from Him. That is good to know. God is still pregnant with many ideas for us. God helps us to bring out His ideas to help people serve their purpose on earth. We are in God, and God is in us. So that means you and I are in the mind of God all the time. God is waiting to spike us out from Himself. Everything starts in the invisible to the visible world. Thank you, God, for being omnipotent and full of purpose and potential. (Now that is good to know.)

God is faith and faith from God to us. God speaks, and faith goes to work for us. Faith comes by hearing and hearing the Word of God. By faith, God speaks, and what He speaks come of Him. Everything is in Him, and all things invisible come visible because God is the word of faith. The idea comes out of God's spirit. Everything starts with God being pregnant with ideas. Every thought I have and you have come from God's idea. That is why we must, as his creation, obey God's plans for our lives. If we do not ask God, we miss the deep things of God.

When you read books and listen to tapes, when you have nothing in your spirit, God's ideas start to come out of Him to you. (God, thank you for your ideas.) By writing this book, this idea comes from God to me, and I act on the invisible, and now it comes out of my spirit and on paper to you. Remember, God creates all things in Himself, and he wants to bring it out of Himself. We are the people of God. He wants to bless us with His ideas. I read in the Bible that faith is not the evidence of things that do not exist but the evidence of things that are not yet seen.

Prophecy—Blessed
(Deuteronomy 28:12–14)

"The Lord shall open unto you his good treasure, the heaven to give the rain unto your land in his season, and to bless all the work of you hand: and you shalt lend not borrow and the Lord shall make you the head, and not the tail; and you shalt be above only, and you shalt not be beneath. If that you hearken unto the commandments of the Lord your God, which I command you this day to observe and to do them."

God has already bought me out from under the curses of the law through Jesus Christ my Lord, for Jesus's blood bought me with a price. The price was Jesus's death, burial, and resurrection and took the keys of death and hell, for Jesus has all power and dominion over the devil and the grave.

"Blessed shalt you be in the city and blessed shalt you be in the field.

"Blessed shat be the fruit of your body, and fruit of your ground, the fruit of your cattle, increase of your children, and flocks of your sheep.

"Blessed shalt be your basket and your store.

"Blessed shalt you be when you come in, blessed shalt you be when you goest out.

"The Lord shalt cause your enemies that rise up against you to be smitten before your face and they that come against you one way, and flee before you seven ways."

(Psalm 1 and all)

(Defeated enemies)

(Psalm 91, Leviticus 26:7–9, Deuteronomy. 28:7, Deuteronomy 32:30, Joshua 1:3, 5–6, 8–9, Psalm 23, Psalm 27:11–14, Psalm 37:3–9, Isaiah 40:3–8, Isaiah 54:14–17, Isaiah 55:3,6–7)

Confessions—All My Needs Meet

"I can do all things through Christ who strengthens me."

"My God shall supply all my need according to God's riches in glory by Christ Jesus."

"Cast not away therefore your confidence, which helps great recompense of reward."

"Casting all my care upon God, for He careth for me [or you]."

"But without faith it is impossible to please God."

"Now faith is the substance of things hoped for, evidence of things not seen."

"Seeing then that we have a great high priest that is passed into heavens, Jesus the Son of God, let us hold fast our profession."

"And this is the confidence that we have in him that if we ask anything according to God will he heareth us."

Thank

Thank you, God, for blessing me with my wife of my youth because "Whoso findeth a wife findeth a good thing and obtaineth favour of the Lord." A virtuous woman is a crown to her husband.

"The fear of the Lord is the beginning of wisdom."

"Husbands, love your wife as Jesus loves the church."

Prayer

Now, heavenly Father, you created my body to function in perfect harmony, and my immune system was intended to protect me from any outside invaders that would cause me harm. God, it is not your will that my immune system is confused and attaching my thyroid gland, and that it is an unhealthy invader. How I thank you for restoring order and peace within my body right now and that all my body systems line up with your Word.

Jesus's name

By Faith

My body was healed of all diseases. I have the mind of Christ.
I have love of God in me.
I have no fear.
I am delivered from sin.
I am delivered from the curse of the law.
I am delivered from familiar spirits. I will prosper in the Lord.
Jesus's name

Say

Now I believe the greater one is in me.

Now I believe He's greater than the devil.

Now I believe He's greater than tests and trials I may face.

I believe He's greater than the storm I may face. He is greater than the problems that may be confronting me.

I believe He's greater than circumstances that seem to have me bound.

I believe He's greater than sickness and disease.

I believe He's greater than anything—everything, and he dwells in me.

Jesus's name

Speak

"God has given me a merry heart doeth good like a medicine."

"A man heart shall be satisfied with good by the fruit of his mouth. The way of the Lord is strength to upright."

"The mouth of the just bring for the wisdom."

"The fear of the Lord is the beginning of wisdom."

"Thy word have I hid in my heart that I might not sin against you."

Three Times Daily

I have strength in my arms.
I have strength in my legs.
I have strength in my fingers.
I have strength in my eyes.
I have strength in my speech.
I have no weakness in my body.
I see clear.
I speak clearly.
I can walk long distances.
Jesus's name

No

No medicine I take will hurt my body.

If we take or drink any deadly thing, it shall not hurt me. For God's Word works like medicine to all my flesh. For with God, nothing shall be impossible to Him.

The Word of God breaks every stronghold of weakness that was in my body—mind. No weapon formed against me shall prosper.

Jesus's name

Shepherd's Door

There is one way to God. It is Jesus. We must come to God by faith that he has given to us. Jesus says, "I am the good shepherd that calls you to the door." God sent Jesus to be the good shepherd that will call and call. Jesus also says, "I am the door of the sheep. I will not let in robbers and thieves but to those who call by faith. Only God can open and close doors for us, and a stranger will I not let in." But he that is hireling, the shepherd will not let them in. (for the wolf) (Jesus will not let them in, for Jesus is the door.)

Potter's Hand

The potter will mold and shape you when we come to Jesus and ask to be used of God. The potter has hands that he used to shape your mind and thoughts. When you study, the Word of God is molding you. Also, the potter has tools. The potter uses a hammer and chisel. Kay, this what the potter uses to hammer the shape of our body and mind. God makes it again, for God is the potter, and the potter can make you again new. The same vessel that was broken— God made it new again, for God is the potter, and we are the work of clay, made new again.

Keeping God's Word

We, as God's people, must ask God to help us keep His Word that is right before Him. Sin separates us from God, and the love is gone.

So when man sins, we have an advocate with the Father and Jesus Christ, the righteous.

God's Word is not old but is new day by day, so let us walk in Him. From the beginning, the new has come the light of men and old passes away. So let us abide in God's Word daily. Write His Word in our heart that we sin not against it.

He who hates his brother is in darkness (sidenote). Love not the world or the things of the world because if so, the lust of the flesh and the eyes and pride of life are in you all. Father looks for people that have their minds stayed on Him.

People need to continue in the faith of God's Word because it will manifest truth to our souls. The unction from the Holy One will show us all the good things to come. Lie not to God and deny not God's Word. So "Whosoever denieth the Son, denieth the Father. But he that acknowledges the Son has the Father also."

The anointing of God will keep you and teach you of His Word. The anointing will not lie but give you the truth of the Word of God, all things it will abide in you to manifest the promise of God.

Call to Set People Free
(Ephesians 4:26–32)

"Be ye angry, and sin not. Let him that stole steal no more. Let no corrupt communication proceed out your mouth. And grieve not the Holy Spirit of God. Let all bitterness, and wrath, and anger, and clamour, and evil speaking, be put away from you with all malice: and be kind one to another, tenderhearted, forgiving one another, even as God for Christ's sake has forgiven you." (Note—speak plainly.)

We must put off the old man and put on the new man that is after God. Former conversation puts it away, and that is old and corrupt according to the deceitful lust of the flesh.

And be renewed in the spirit of your mind that we put on the new man which God created in righteousness and true holiness.

"For no man ever yet hated his own self, but nourisheth and cherished it, even as the Lord the church. For we are members of His body (the church). For we are members of His body, of His flesh and bones." (Note—speak plainly.)

Fellowship with God

John 1: 1–10—God will manifest himself to us when we come to him because light and darkness cannot be in the same place where God is. How can we say we have fellowship with Him if we walk in lies of our confession? We cannot.

The fellowship of God drives out the darkness because the light comes to us from God's Word. God wants us to come to him with all our cares of life. So let us walk with God in the light.

Our fellowship with God is so powerful that God says, "If we lie, we walk in darkness, and the truth is not in us." God's Word is the light.

God will manifest Himself to us when we walk in His will—the Word. Why? Because God is light. Confession is made unto God.

Confession is good. We get all things out before God, and He can clean us up (washed by the blood of Jesus.) So let us not deceived ourselves. What a man sow shall he reap. So sin kills, but God's Word makes us alive.

I will bring all my tithes and offerings into God's house that there be meat in my house, and the Lord will open up the heaven and pour me out a blessing. And the Lord will rebuke the devourer for my sake, and the devil shall not destroy the fruit of my ground. My vine shall not cast her fruit before the time in the field said the Lord of hosts. And all nations shall call us blessed and delightsome land.

"Hear me, Lord, when I call, O God of my righteousness. You had enlarged me when I was in distress. Have mercy upon me and hear my prayer.

"Give ear to my words, O Lord, consider my meditation. Hearken unto the voice of my cry, my King and God: for unto you will I cry.

"My voice shalt you hear in the morning, O Lord; in the morning will I direct my prayer unto you, and will look up."

The Lord has heard my supplication. The Lord will receive my prayer.

Hear the right, O Lord. Attend unto my cry. Give ear unto my prayer that not out of feigned lips.

Prophecy—Give Me

I have anointed you.
I have called you.
I have a good work in you.
You are a speaking spirit.
You are a son of God.
Jesus begot you.
Jesus has redeemed you.

Book

Surely, the words that we speak out of our mouths can heal or kill. Sometimes, we all make the mistake of saying the wrong things out of the heart. Be sure God will hear only positive, not negative, which word will God respond to. Remember, your words are the healing of your body and mind. So look at some words that we speak every day and see if they will help us or hinder you.

Will

God's Word is His will. So if you do not have the Word of God with you, how are you going to know God's will? Some people come to church and have their Bible not with them or have it on the floor or beside them—not even picking up the will, which is the Word to see what His will is for their lives. Why is this so hard for people who say they believe in God? I know my will, which is my word. Without it, how can you know right from wrong thinking? People write a will for their family, and they give it to the law. So when they die, the family may have something to fall back on. So if they do not open the will and read the will that was left behind, how would they know what is in it for them? That is the same thing I am saying to you.

Pick up the Word, which is God's will for your life, and learn what is in the will. Jesus left it for you, and what is in there is all for the taking. It is wrong for you not to know the will, the Word that can and will save your soul from hellfire. God calls you to know it, and know it now, right now. The devil is killing people who do not know the will. He left for you. The devil is breaking families apart, and men and women are now committing adultery and fornication. So if you do not read the will, which is the Word, how can you know this is wrong to do. People are dying because of a lack of knowledge of His will. Come and learn with me. I am open to teaching you all you need to know.

Spirit of Trust (John 4)

1. Love one another.
2. Every spirit that confesseth that Jesus Christ is cometh in the flesh is of God.
3. God's little children have overcome them.
4. Greater is He that is in you than He that is in the world.
5. We are of God. He that heard us heareth God.
6. For God is love—love is God.
7. In this was manifested the love of God toward us, God sent His only begotten son into the world.
8. God sent His Son to be the propitiation for our sins.
9. We ought also to love one another.
10. God dwelleth in us, and His love is perfected in us.
11. God knows we dwell in Him, and He has given us His spirit.
12. We do testify the Father sent His Son to be our Savior of the world.
13. Whosoever shall confess Jesus is the Son of God, and He is God.
14. He that dwelleth in love dwelleth in God, and God is in him.
15. We have boldness in that day of judgment.
16. Because so as He is, so are we in this world.
17. Perfect love casteth out fear.
18. We love Him because He first loved us.
19. He who loveth God love his brother also.

Spirit of Error (John 4)

1. Every spirit that confesseth not Jesus Christ come in the flesh is not of God.
2. They speak of the world, and the world hears them.
3. He that heareth not us hear not God.
4. He that heareth not God heareth not us.
5. He that loveth not knoweth not God, for God is love.
6. There is no fear in love.
7. Because fear hath torment, he that feareth is not made perfect in love.
8. If a man says, "I love God and hateth his brother," he is a liar, and the truth is not in him.
9. How can he see his brother and hate him whom he sees and yet whom he cannot seeth say he loves God who can't see?

Tongue

James 3:1–5—the tongue can speak good or evil. It can set the course of heaven or hell. That how powerful the tongue can be in your life. The tongue is a small member of the body but can boast great things or small things. It is up to you to control the tongue and what comes out of it. Then it is put bits in the horse's mouth or your mouth that there may be self-control in your life. The world speaks of iniquity and will defile your body (the whole body). "Every kind of beast, and of birds, and of serpents, and of things in the sea, is tamed, and hath been tamed of mankind." But the tongue cannot be tamed by man. It is an unruly evil, full of deadly poison. So out of the same mouth proceedeth blessing and cursing. But when we renew your mind in God's Word, God can change our speech. The Word of God will change the way we talk and think, for out of the heart, the mouth speaks.

Look at James 3:17. "Who is a wise man and endued with knowledge? let him shew out of a good conversation his work with meekness of wisdom." But if you have better envying and strife in your heart, how can we speak good things out of our mouth and lie not against the truth? It says, "This wisdom descends not from above, but it is earthly, sensual, devilish. For where envying and strife is confusion and every evil work. But the wisdom that is from above is first pure, then peaceable, gentle, and easy to be entreated, full of mercy and good fruits." So when we renew our mind, then the fruit of righteousness is sown in peace of them that makes peace.

Potter's Wheel

Jeremiah 18:1–6—Go down to the potter's house and get a word from God. For God, who formed you by His hand, He will shape you in what He wants you to be. God will keep you on the wheel until He finishes with you. God will mold and shape your mind and body.

The longer you stay on the wheel, the longer God can shape you in what He wants you to be, spinning you around and around.

Let God work and work in you. Let go, and let God finish you with His hand. I will be what God wants me to be in Him. Do not let God stop working on you. Let God finish working on areas of your life.

You are the created vessel of God that he made of clay, as seemed good to the potter to make it.

The vessel is made by God's hand, for the potter knows the vessel he made of clay.

God makes new clay and makes vessels by the old clay. Only a master can make a new vessel for His work. God changes me from an old into a new vessel.

God has the grace to change you that is old by the mercy of God into the new vessel you are today.

Because you have been redeemed by the Lord, the new vessel of clay has been redeemed by God's grace.

All Spirits Are Subjected to God

Saul had an evil spirit that tormented his mind and thoughts, but his servant, David, had the talent in music to temporarily help Saul's condition.

In your life, you have an evil spirit that easily besets you. There are good spirits and evil spirits that stay around us all the time, but we must discern between the two. In 1 Corinthians 12:10, it says, "To another discerning of spirits."

We are in a warfare every day. In 2 Corinthians 10:4, it says, "For the weapons of our warfare are not carnal, but mighty through God to pulling down of strongholds."

Did Saul go to God about his tormenting spirit, or did he ask for help? No, but his servant did. They went about to seek out help for the king. David was the answer for a short time, but God was the ultimate answer.

What we can do in going to God can help us in our lives to overcome these spirits. In 2 Corinthians 10:5, it says, "Casting down imaginations and every high thing that exalteth itself against the knowledge of God." Get your mind on something else. When the evil thoughts come, speak the Word out of your mouth. "Bringing into captivity every thought to the obedience of Christ."

Hidden Potential

I will not die with my potential inside of me. God gave every man and woman gifts, abilities, wealth, and successes hidden down within us. I will not go to the grave with my potential in me and not bring it out for God to use and people to be blessed by it. God helps me to bring out the hidden potential that He has given me to maximize my life.

O Lord God, help me not to die with your purpose that you gave me to live out this life. I have books and songs that need to come out of my mouth. O Lord God, help me to release your ability before I come to heaven. I believe I have books and songs and poems down in me, and the seed has to die and grow to its potential. I will not give up until my purpose and potential come out of me.

God creates life into something called man. God loves us so much He created His own life into something called man. That is how deep God's love is to us. God loves us that he sends Jesus to pay the price to redeem us back to God our Father, know that His love that no man can comprehend. Know that it is good to know. Psalm 16 reads, "I love the Lord because he hath heard my voice and my supplications. Because he has inclined his ear unto me, therefore will I call upon him as long as I live."

Tossed

Do not waver like some do, but be steadfast in what you know is true in God's Word, for it shall come to pass in your life.

"Whatever you ask in my name, I will give it to you when you ask of me. But when the wind drives you, stand still for it shall blow over you, for I, the Lord God, will cause it to blow pass all your problems in life. Be still. Wait for me to move you out. Keep your mind on me. Receive not the fresh things of this world. Wait. Let your mind stays on my word day and night, for you shall receive of me if you keep my word."

You will not fade when you keep the order. The man that endures temptation will receive the crown of righteousness, which the Lord has promised to them that love him.

For temptation is not of God but of the lust and enticed that a man has in him for God cannot tempt with evil. God is love. "When lust hath conceived, it bringeth forth sin: and when it is finished, bringeth forth death." God wants you to live and not die.

God gives every man a gift, and that gift is perfect from above. "For Father cometh down from heaven has light to all men to see his love that cannot be moved neither shadow of turning. For God begot us with his word of truth. For we are of the firstfruits of his creatures."

Prayer of Fruit

The fruit of the spirit is love, joy, peace, long-suffering, gentleness, goodness, faith, meekness, and temperance. It overrules bitterness and fear because bitterness and fear are not of the fruit of the spirit, for I believe that I have the fruit of God working in me at all times. God, I thank you for destroying the spirit of fear and bitterness in my heart. I will operate in love that you have given me in my life right now in Jesus's name.

The fruit of the spirit gives me the patience, and patience has her perfect work in me at all times. I will ask in faith not wavering for he that wavers is double-minded and unstable in all his ways.

I will receive the newness of life in Christ Jesus. Bitterness and fear will not have dominion over me. I have dominion over fear and bitterness because I have the fruit of the spirit working in me at all times.

I believe and receive dominion overall fear and bitterness in my life for love, joy, peace, long-suffering, gentleness, goodness, faith, meekness, and temperance are working in my life right now. In Jesus's name.

Health—Healing

Psalm 30:2—O Lord, my God, I cried unto you, and you have healed me.

Psalm 41:4—I said, "Lord, be merciful unto me, heal my soul."

Psalm 42:11—For I shall yet praise him who is the health of my countenance and my God.

Psalm 103:3—Forgiveth all my iniquities, who healeth all my disease.

Psalm 102:22—He sent his Word and healed me and delivered me from all their destructions.

Proverbs 4:22—For they are life unto those that find me and health to all me fresh.

Proverbs 12:18—But the tongue of the wise is health.

Proverbs 13:17—But a faithful ambassador is health.

Proverbs 18:13—A merry heart maketh a cheerful countenance.

Proverbs 16:24—Pleasant words are a honeycomb, sweet to the soul and health to the bones.

Proverbs 17:22—A merry heart doeth good like a medicine.

Isaiah 53:4–5—Jesus hath borne our grief and carried our sorrows. We esteemed him stricken, smitten of God, and afflicted. Jesus was wounded for our transgressions. Jesus was bruised for our iniquities. Jesus's chastisement of our peace was upon Jesus, and with Jesus's stripes, we are healed.

God Is True Light of Confession

1. Your word, O Lord, is a lamp unto my feet and a light unto my path. I have sworn the Lord, and I will perform it.
2. The entrance of my words giveth light. It giveth understanding unto the unlearned.
3. Open my mouth, O Lord, and help me plant seeds of righteousness.
4. Order my steps in your word, and let not any iniquity have dominion over me.
5. I cried with my whole heart. Hear me, O Lord, and I will keep thy commandments.
6. Let my cry come near before you, O Lord. Give me understanding according to your word.
7. Let my supplication come before you. Deliver me according to thy word. My lips shall utter praise when you hast taught me your commandments. My tongue shall speak of your word for all your commandments are righteousness. Let thine hand help me, for I have chosen your precepts.
8. I have longed for your salvation, O Lord, and your word is my delight. Let my soul live, O Lord, and it shall praise you and let your judgments help me.
9. The power of God that is in me has healed all weaknesses in my arms and legs.
10. Jesus has given me dominion over all weapons of the devil—the enemy of faith.
11. Through faith, my confidence rest in Jesus, for Jesus has given me victory in all the promises of God.
12. I believe God's promise of a divine reward of diligently seeking Him.

13. The Word of God is quick and powerful than any two-edged sword, for God's Word is a discerner of thoughts and intents of the heart.
14. God said, "Resist the devil, and he will run from the presence of God's power that is in you."
15. Cast not away therefore your confidence, which has great recompense of reward. Because without faith, it is impossible to please Him.
16. Let all draw near to Him with a true heart in the full assurance of faith in receiving His promises.
17. For this is the covenant that I make with you, my children. I will put my word in your spirit and mind, for you are my people.
18. For Jesus is my mediator of the New Testament, which we are the people to receive the promise of eternal life.
19. For God swore by none other than Himself saying surely blessing, "I will bless you with all the promise of health and strength that is in me."
20. Today, if we hear God calling us to repent, harden not your heart, for God wants to bless you with eternal life.
21. For which cause we faint not. God looketh at the inward man, not at outward man.
22. These are light afflictions to the inward man. For the outward man perish, yet the inward man is renewed day by day in the spirit.
23. We have the same faith. Our spirit is quickened by hearing and hearing the Word of God.
24. How can we hear if we have not preacher to tell us? God's Word shines a light into the dark places in our lives.
25. For we walk by faith and not by sight. Because without faith, it is impossible to please God. For God is a spirit, and all who call on Him must first believe in Him.
26. But, beloved, be not ignorant of this one thing. One day with God is a thousand years and a thousand years as one day with God.

27. Jesus Christ is our Savior. For all those who call on Him will be saved from eternal death.

28. For God so loved the world that He gave his only Son to us that who will call on Him will not perish but have everlasting life.

29. He that believes in Him is not condemned. The light has come, and darkness is gone.

30. That which is born of the flesh is flesh, and that which is born of the spirit of God is a spirit from above.

31. Verily I say unto you, except a man be born again, he cannot see the kingdom of God.

32. The spirit of God bloweth on who he will so is every one that is born of the spirit of God.

33. Jesus came down from heaven that we may ascend up to heaven that calls on His name.

34. But he that doeth the truth cometh to the light, that his deeds are manifest to God the Father.

And

God said, "Let there be light," and there was light.

God said, "Let there be a firmament in the midst of the waters, and let it divide the waters from the waters."

God said, "Let the waters under the heavens be gathered together unto one place, and let the dry land appear," and it was so.

God said, "Let the earth bring forth grass, herb yielding seed, and fruit tree yielding fruit after his own kind, whose seed is in itself upon the earth," and it was so.

God said, "Let there be lights in the firmament of the heaven to divide the day from the night, and let them be for signs, and for seasons, and for days, and years."

God said, "Let the waters bring forth abundantly the moving creature that has life and fowl that may fly above the earth in the open firmament of heaven."

God said, "Let the earth bring forth the living creature after his kind, cattle, creeping thing, beast of the earth after his kind," and it was so.

God said, "Let us make man in our image, after our likeness, and let them have dominion over the fish of the sea, over the fowl of the air, over the cattle, over all the earth, over creepeth upon the earth."

God blessed them, and God said unto them, "Be fruitful and multiply and replenish the earth and subdue it."

God said, "Behold I have given you every herb bearing seed, which is upon the face of all the earth, and every tree in the which is the fruit of a tree yielding seed to you it shall be for meat."

God saw everything that he had made and behold it was very good, and the evening and the morning were the sixth day.

God blessed the seventh day and sanctified it because that in it He rested from all His work which God created and made.

Work It Out

"The eyes of the Lord are upon the righteous, and His ear is open to their cry."

"Ask, and it shall be given to you; seek, and you shall find; knock, and it shall be opened unto you."

"Give not that which is holy unto the dogs, neither cast your pearls before swine."

"But seek first the kingdom of God and His righteousness, and all these things shall be added unto you."

"No man can serve two masters, for either he will hate the one and love the other. You cannot serve God and mammon."

"For there is no respect of persons with God."

"Work out your own salvation with fear and trembling."

"Being confident of this very thing, that he [God] which hath begun a good work in you will perform it until the day of Jesus Christ."

Prayer of Salvation

Dear heavenly Father, I thank you for sending Jesus Christ into the world to give His life for my sins on the cross. I acknowledge to you, Father, that I am a sinner and that I confess with my mouth and believe in my heart that Jesus Christ is and now is my Lord and Savior, and according to His Word, right now, I am born-again.

The Books That Helped Me to Grow

In strength are Matthew, Luke, Corinthians, Romans, James, Peter, John, Psalm 1, Proverbs, Isaiah, and Habakkuk. I read to strengthen me in walking closer with God. It is good to know that the Word of God can inspire us to grow in our faith and change and challenge us in life. Matthew 18:3–4 says, "Verily I say unto you, except you be converted, and become as little children, you shall not enter into the kingdom of heaven. Whosoever therefore shall humble himself as this little child, the same is greatest in the kingdom of heaven."

I have to come as a little child to be healed and delivered from many wrong things I thought was to be right in my eyes. But God always has a perfect plan for our lives if we just look to Him. If we take a note out of Jesus's life, we all may be better off. Live out His life than I own lives. Well, here we go. Get ready to be blessed.

Quiet Time Study

Prepared the Way	Conquerors	Call to Fellowship
Matt. 16:20-28	Romans 14:16-23	Psalms 51:All
Matt. 17:1-5	Psalms 91:10-12	1 John 1:7
Matt. 5:14-17	2 Thess. 3:10	1 Corinth. 1:2-3
Malachi 4:5-6	Psalms 19:6-14	Phillip. 1:1-2
Matt. 11:1-16	Deut. 6:13-15	Phillip. 4:4,8,13,17,19
Isaiah 40:3-8	1 Corinth. 10:13	Ephesians 1:5-14
Luke 3:4-9	1 Corinth. 6:13	
Proverbs 28:9	James 4:7-8	
Luke 18:9-14	Romans 8:37-39	
Luke 12:13-17		
Isaiah 6:1-8		

Heirs of God	Witness	Charity Never Faileth
Galatians 4:4-7	Acts 8:All	1 Corinth. 11:23-29
Romans 8:11-17	Hebrew 11:7	2 Corinth. 13:3-8
John 1:12-13	Genesis 6:1-9	Galatians 4:4-7
Romans 10:17	John 5:39	John 3:18
Luke 8:4-18	John 5:9-10	Isaiah 60:1-5
Hebrew 12:1-3	Colossians 2:9-11	Galatians 3:22-29
Matt. 3:7-17	Matt. 24:3-39	Galatians 5:6
Matt. 4:1-11	1 Corinth. 10:31-33	Ephesians 3:1-12
	1 Thess. 4:14-18	Ephesians 3:14-19
		John 4:7-12

Gave Himself	Spirit Wash Us	If My People
Ephesians 5:25-33	Rev. 1:1-5	2 Chron. 7:12-16
Genesis 1:26	Acts 19:1-6	2 Corinth. 4:16-18
1 Corinth. 5:45-49	Acts 8:26-40	2 Corinth. 10:3-6
Romans 5:14	Rev. 5-6	Ephesians 6:10-19
Genesis 2:18-25	2 Chron. 9:17-21	Hebrew 4:12-16
Ephesians 5:22-33	Romans 8:1-2	1 Peter 4:11-19
Genesis 5:1-2	1 Corinth. 10:13	2 Corinth. 12:1-12
Ephesians 5:20, 25	Galatians 5:16-17	Romans 5:1-5
1 Corinth. 10:17	1 Corinth. 13:1-8	2 Corinth. 4:7-10
John 19:31-37		Acts 5:29-32
John 3:1-8, 15		1 Timothy 3:1-15
1 John 5:1-18		Isaiah 55:6-17

The Word Made Flesh	Watch What You Say	Stand
Ephesians 3:16-22	2 Corinth. 5:17	Zech. 12:9-10
1 John 5:1-12	Romans 8:1-6	Ephesians 6:10-19
Rev. 12:11	Hebrew 11:1-3	Galatians 5:1-2
Rev. 19:13	Psalms 18:21-22	Romans 8:26-28
Exodus 17:11	James 3:1-15	1 Corinth. 14:1-5
John 1:14	Mark 11:22-24	1 Corinth. 1:4-7

1 John 1:6-8	Matt. 12:31-37	Jude 1:20-21
Psalms 119:105-130	Romans 10:8	Ezekiel 36:24-30
Phillip. 2:1-4	Romans 4:16-21	1 Corinth. 14:8-17
Psalms 33:18-22	Hebrew 3:1-8	1 Corinth. 14:39-40
1 Peter 2:24	Hebrew 4:14-16	

Faith Cometh	Unspeakable Words	Sign
Hebrew 11:6	Rev. 1:1-5	Isaiah 7:14
Romans 10;17	1 Corinth. 12:1-10	Genesis 22:7
Proverbs 4:20-22	Rev. 1:11	John 3:14-17
Proverbs 3:5-6	Rev. 1:7-20	Phillip. 2:5-7
2 Corinth. 3:6	John 1:1-10	Phillip. 2:13-16
Isaiah 55:8-13	Exodus 25:31-40	Hebrew 2:3-9
Matt. 15:21-29	Matt. 5:14-16	Isaiah 9:6-7
Luke 1:3-38		
Luke 1:45		
Matt. 7:All		
James 1:1-2		
Isaiah 54:2		
Isaiah 49:18-23		

And Be Not	Word Revealed to Gentiles	Preach
Romans 12:1-2	Acts 10:11-19	Rev. 22:18-19
Hebrews 8:1-8	Ephesians 3:6-11	John 15:1-6
Colossians 2:18-23	John 10:1-5	Ezekiel 3:1-3
Psalms 14:8-14	Ephesians 4:1-7	Mark 16:15
1 Samuel 13:1-10	Acts 15:12-26	John 20:30-31
1Corinth. 10:12-18	Ephesians 2:10-13	Rev. 1:1-4
Leviticus 10:All	Mark 3:17	Romans 8:26
2 Corinth. 10:3-6	Ephesians 6:1-3	Hebrew 9:27-28
	John 13:21-30	Phillip. 2:8-13
	1 Corinth. 13:1-7	Acts 19:All
	Rev. 2:1-7	Rev. 2:1-29
		Acts 17:6-11

Church	God Foreknew	His Coming
Rev. 3:1-6	John 13:1-11, 18-30	Acts 17:24-34
2 Chron. 16:9	Ephesians 1:5-11	Matt. 24:24
Rev. 6-10	Romans 8:28-30	Exodus 34:14-15
Zech. 4:1-6	Genesis 1:26-27	Rev. 2:18-29
Rev. 3:4-13	Genesis 2:16-17	Jeremiah 3:13-18
Ephesians 4:8-10	Romans 8:8	Ezekiel 16:1-4
2 Corinth. 12:1-4	John 5:13-14	Hosea 2:1-7
Colossians 2:13-15	Colossians 2:20-23	Acts 16:9-15
	Rev. 22:17	Rev. 2:20-23
	John 5:40-41	2 King 9:22
	2 Peter 3:9	1 King 18:4, 12
	Romans 6:16-18	1 King 21:1-11

	2 Corinth. 10:All 2 Timothy 2:16-21 Mark 16:15-20	Rev. 2:26-29 Rev. 17:All
Fellowship	**Thief**	**Time of the End**
Galatians 3:7-14	John 10:10-18	Daniel 12:3-4
Galatians 5:6-13	John 3:3-15	Acts 2:14-21
Luke 8:22-25	Acts 2: 1-5, 15:19	Acts 2:37-39
1 John 1:6-18	Psalms 37:3, 8-9, 11	1 Corinth. 1:4-10
John 15:All	Galatians 5:16	1 Corinth. 13:8-13
	Isaiah 40:28-31	2 Corinth. 10:3-6
	Phillip. 4:4-8, 13, 19	Hebrew 5:12-14
		1 Corinth. 2:11-16
		1 Corinth 3:1-8
		Rev. 3:3-5

About the Author

First and foremost, Covell Johnson is a Christian born in Washington, DC, and raised with five brothers and three sisters. His father and mother raised them to be the best Christian family they can be, to work hard, provide for their children, learn more about God, Father, Jesus his Son, and Holy Spirit. He is a born-again Christian, and Jesus Christ is his Lord and Savior.

Printed in the USA
CPSIA information can be obtained
at www.ICGtesting.com
LVHW041535020124
767910LV00001B/364